Raw Vegan Soups

Delicious and Nutritious Raw Food Soup Recipes

By: Kevin Kerr

2 Raw Vegan Soups

Table of Contents

6 Raw Vegan Soups

Introduction

First off, all of these recipes would be impossible to make without a blender. All soups serve 1 to 3 people. Feel free to garnish with your favorite dried or fresh herbs, soaked nuts, diced vegetables, or fruit. Out of the listed ingredients for each soup you can choose not to blend the ones you want to save for your garnish. If your heart desires a warm soup then you can lightly heat over the stove, use hot water in the recipe, or blend using the soup mode on your high speed blender. Aside from tasting better, being better for your body, and being cruelty-free; uncooked vegan soups take less prep time. I personally love these recipes and use one or more every day. Raw soups are so beneficial for the human body because they practically digest themselves. Raw food is anything that isn't heated over 118 degrees so that the precious enzymes aren't destroyed. In order for food to digest it must be broken down by enzymes. Science has recently discovered that our bodies can only produce so many enzymes in this lifetime which is the number one reason to eat as much raw food as you enjoy. A great way to start is by trying the soups!

Herbal Green Pea
- 2 cups peas
- 1 avocado
- 1 ½ cups almond milk
- ½ cup fresh basil
- ½ small red onion
- ½ cup fresh chives
- 1 clove garlic
- sea salt to taste

Spicy Cucumber Cabbage
- 2 large cucumbers
- 3 cabbage leaves
- 1 (hot) pepper of choice
- 1 small heirloom tomato
- 2 tablespoons olive oil
- pink Himalayan salt to taste

Mexican Fiesta

- 2 medium heirloom tomatoes
- 2 red bell peppers
- 8 sun dried tomatoes
- 8 sprigs of fresh cilantro
- 2 stalks celery
- 1 cup water
- fresh squeeze lime juice
- ½ avocado
- 2 tbsp. cold-pressed olive oil
- 1 clove garlic
- ¼ tsp. cumin
- ½ tsp. chili or cayenne powder
- ½ teaspoon paprika
- sea salt to taste

Sea Soup Specialty

- 3 cups zucchini noodles made with spiralizer (add in whole after soup is blended)
- 3 nori sheets
- 1 tsp. dulse
- ½ tsp. kelp granules
- 2 tbsp. coconut oil
- 2 cups hot water or your favorite tea

Tomato Basil

- 3 medium heirloom tomatoes
- 4 sun dried tomatoes
- 2 stalks celery
- small chunk of red onion
- ½ clove fresh garlic
- 5 leaves fresh basil
- ½ avocado
- sea salt to taste

Cream of Cucumber

- 2 large cucumbers (peel and all if organic)
- ½ cup macadamia nuts
- squeeze of fresh lemon juice
- 1 clove garlic
- 1 avocado
- 1 cup of water
- sea salt to taste

Cream of Tomato
- 2 large heirloom tomatoes
- 3 stalks celery
- 1 medium carrot
- 1 clove garlic
- juice of 1 lemon
- ½ cup raw cashews
- 1 avocado
- 1 orange bell pepper
- 2 pitted dried medjool dates (optional)
- ½ tsp. cumin
- 5 sprigs cilantro
- 1 tbsp. soaked pumpkin seeds
- pink Himalayan salt to taste

Cream of Nectarine
- 7 to 8 peeled and pitted nectarines (depending on size)
- 2 cups spinach
- ½ cup water
- ½ tsp. cinnamon

Cream of Mango

- 3 cups fresh mango
- 1 cup coconut milk
- 1 tbsp. coconut cream
- 2 tbsp. coconut sugar
- 3 leaves fresh mint
- 3 leaves fresh spearmint

Cream of Carrot

- 2 large carrots
- 1 cup macadamia nuts
- 1 clove garlic
- 1 tbsp. raw apple cider vinegar
- 3 green onions
- 1 red bell pepper
- sea salt to taste

Green Goodness

- 1 cucumber (peel and all if organic)
- 1 cup spinach
- 1 orange bell pepper
- 1 avocado
- 1 tbsp. raw tahini
- juice of 1 lemon
- sea salt to taste

Fennel Basil Tomato Soup

- 1 fennel bulb
- 1 cup water
- 2 medium heirloom tomatoes
- ½ cup fresh basil
- ½ yellow bell pepper
- fresh squeeze lime juice
- sea salt to taste

Cream of Lime

- 2 avocados
- juice of 2 small limes (or 1 large)
- 3 sprigs fresh cilantro
- ½ cup fresh chives
- 1 tsp. cumin
- 1 stalk celery
- 1 cup water
- sea salt to taste

Cream of Celery

- 7 stalks celery
- ½ cup raw cashews
- 1 avocado
- 1 clove garlic
- 1 cup water
- kala namak salt to taste

Cream of Zucchini

- 3 cups zucchini (peel and all if organic)
- 1 cup peas
- 2 stalks celery
- 1 avocado
- 1 cup water
- juice of 1 lemon
- 2 cloves fresh garlic
- 1 tsp. fresh thyme
- 1 tsp. turmeric
- pinch of cayenne pepper
- sea salt to taste

Cream of Pumpkin

- 1 cup pumpkin (seeds and skin removed)
- 2 pitted dried medjool dates
- 1 cup raw cashews
- ¼ tsp. cinnamon
- sea salt to taste

Green Onion Tomato Soup

- 2 large heirloom tomatoes
- 1 yellow bell pepper
- 3 green onions
- 1 cucumber
- 1 clove garlic
- ½ small red onion
- sea salt to taste

Cream of Spinach

- 2 cups spinach
- 1 cup water
- 1 cup macadamia nuts
- 4 green onions
- 1 clove garlic
- ½ tsp nutmeg
- sea salt to taste

Carrot Ginger Soup

- 2 large carrots
- 1 thumb-sized piece of ginger
- 2 tbsp. black sesame seeds
- 2 pitted dried medjool dates
- pinch of black or cayenne pepper
- ½ tsp. turmeric
- 2 cups water
- sea salt to taste

Cream of Broccoli

- 1 head of broccoli (excluding stalk)
- 2 stalks celery
- 1 clove garlic
- ½ small red onion
- fresh squeeze lemon juice
- tsp. dried oregano
- 1 cup water
- pinch of black pepper
- ½ tsp turmeric
- kala namak salt to taste

Garden Blend

- 1 zucchini (peel and all if organic)
- 2 medium heirloom tomatoes
- 2 stalks celery
- 2 medium carrots
- 1 clove garlic
- 2 pitted dried medjool dates
- 1 cup water
- 2 tbsp. olive oil
- pinch of black pepper
- 1 tsp. turmeric
- sea salt to taste

Cream of Cauliflower

- 4 cups cauliflower
- 1 cup soaked raw almonds
- 1 tsp. olive oil
- 1 tsp. coconut oil
- 1 cup arugula
- ½ tsp. rosemary
- sea salt to taste

Strawberry Beet Soup
- 10 whole strawberries (including green tops)
- 2 small beets
- 2 cups water
- 3 green onions
- sea salt to taste

Spicy Lime Soup
- 1 stalk celery
- 1 cup yellow squash
- juice of 1 lime
- 1 chili pepper
- 2 medium carrots
- 2 small heirloom tomatoes
- 1 cup zucchini
- 1 cup cabbage
- 1 clove garlic
- 1 cup water
- sea salt to taste

Carrot Soup

- 1 whole head of broccoli
- 2 medium carrots
- 1 medium heirloom tomato
- ½ zucchini
- 5 raw brazil nuts
- 1 cup water
- sea salt to taste

Cream of Lemon

- 1 lemon (peel and all if organic)
- 1 small heirloom tomato
- 1 avocado
- ¼ cup olive oil
- ½ cup fresh parsley
- 4 stalks celery
- 1 tsp. maple syrup
- 3 cups water
- sea salt to taste

Cream of Mushroom

- 8 oz. of your favorite mushrooms
- 2 cups water
- 4 green onions
- ½ cup cashews
- ¼ cup pine nuts
- ¼ cup hazelnuts
- 4 sprigs fresh parsley
- sea salt to taste

Cream of Cabbage

- 2 cups cabbage
- 2 cups peas
- 1 avocado
- ½ zucchini (peel and all if organic)
- 1 stalk celery
- 1 tbsp. chia seeds
- ½ small red onion
- sea salt to taste

Cream of Pumpkin

- 2 cups pumpkin
- 2 cups water
- 2 cups cauliflower
- ½ cup pecans
- ½ tsp. mustard powder
- 1 tsp. cumin
- 3 sprigs cilantro
- sea salt to taste

Winter Specialty Soup

- 2 cups water
- 3 cups pumpkin
- 1 small carrot
- 2 green onions
- 1 stalk celery
- 1 cup kale
- 1 thumb-sized chunk of ginger
- 1 clove garlic
- 1 avocado
- 1 chili pepper
- sea salt to taste

Thai Ginger Soup

- 2 cups water
- ½ red bell pepper
- 1 small carrot
- 1 stalk celery
- 1 acorn squash
- 3 green onions
- fresh squeeze lemon juice
- 1 small apple
- ½ cup cashews
- 1 thumb-sized chunk of ginger
- 1 clove garlic
- 3 sprigs cilantro
- sea salt to taste

Cooling Watermelon Soup

- 3 cups watermelon
- juice of 1 lime
- 1 small cucumber (peel and all if organic)
- ½ cup fresh mint

Vegan Heaven Soup

- 2 cups water
- 2 cups broccoli
- 2 stalks celery
- 2 green onions
- ½ cup cashews
- 1 clove garlic
- 1 sprig fresh rosemary
- 1 sprig fresh lime
- sea salt to taste

Light Lettuce Soup

- ½ lb. romaine lettuce
- 2 cups peas
- 2 green onions
- 1 cup water
- sea salt to taste

Belly Buster Soup
- 1 small raw sweet potato
- 2 cups water
- 1 cup pumpkin
- 1 red bell pepper
- 1 stalk celery
- 1 medium carrot
- 1 green onion
- 1 small heirloom tomato
- 1 cup cabbage
- sea salt to taste

Cream of Pepper
- 1 red bell pepper
- 1 clove garlic
- 1 avocado
- 1 large heirloom tomato
- ½ small red onion
- 1 tsp. cumin
- sea salt to taste

Wonderland Soup

- 2 cups swiss chard
- 3 cups water
- 1 small carrot
- 1 stalk celery
- 2 green onions
- ½ cup brazil nuts
- 1 clove garlic
- squeeze of fresh lime juice
- ½ tsp. turmeric
- pinch of black pepper
- sea salt to taste

Cream of Chestnut

- 2 cups water
- ½ cup chestnuts
- 2 large carrots
- 1 stalk celery
- 1 sprig of parsley, rosemary and thyme
- 2 basil leaves
- sea salt to taste

Exquisite Tomato Soup
- 1 cup brazil nut milk
- 1 cup water
- 1 large heirloom tomato
- ½ cup sun dried tomatoes
- 1 red bell pepper
- 1 stalk celery
- ½ small red onion
- ¼ cup cashews
- 1 small carrot
- ¼ cup fresh basil
- 1 clove garlic
- pinch of cayenne pepper
- 1 tsp. oregano
- 2 tbsps. lemon juice
- sea salt to taste

Cream of Corn
- 2 cups raw corn
- ¼ cup cashews
- 1 cup water
- 1 clove garlic
- sea salt to taste

Printed in France by Amazon
Brétigny-sur-Orge, FR

15170884R00016